The Best I Can Be

BERT ROBBINS

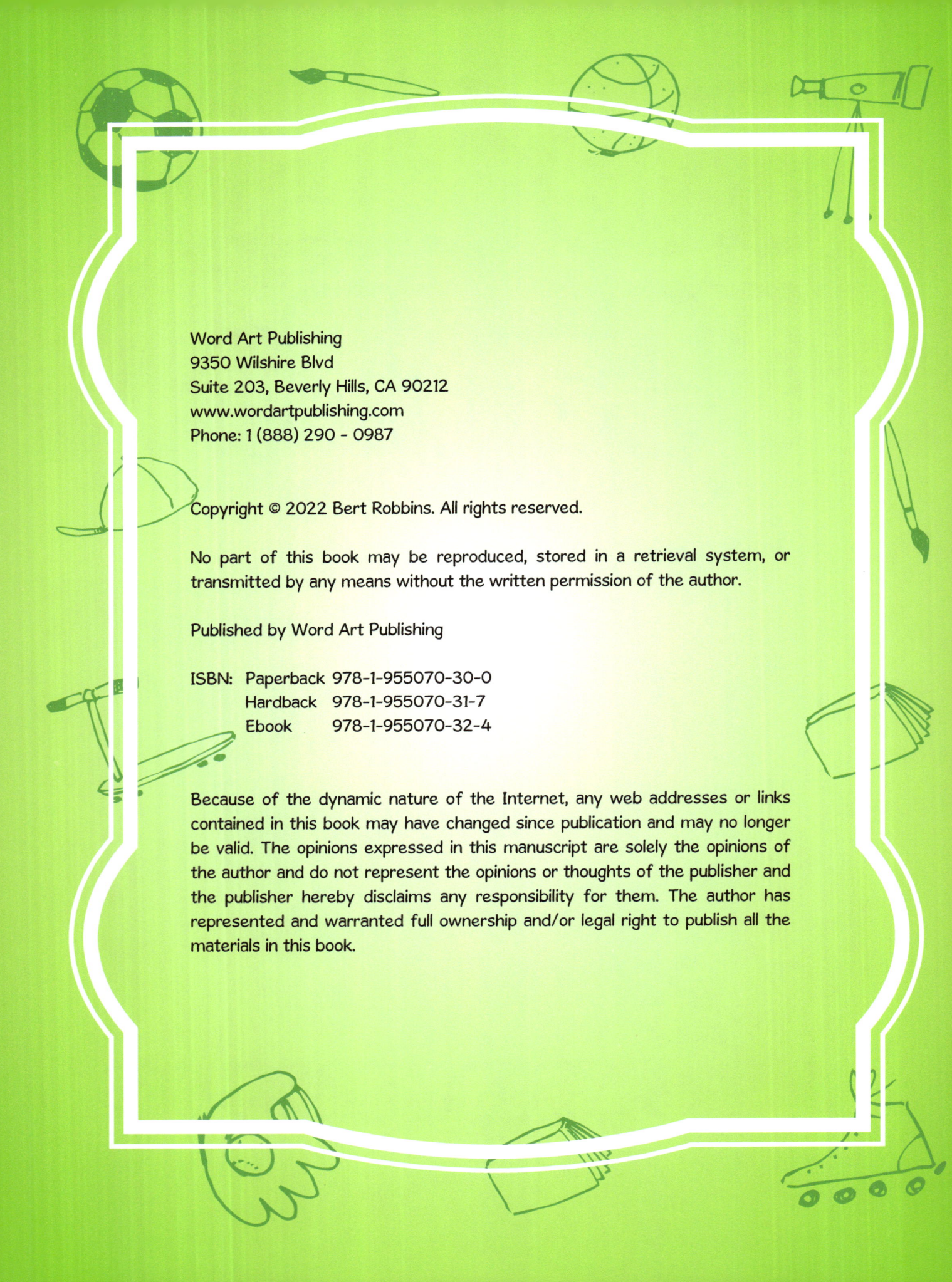

Word Art Publishing
9350 Wilshire Blvd
Suite 203, Beverly Hills, CA 90212
www.wordartpublishing.com
Phone: 1 (888) 290 - 0987

Published by Word Art Publishing

ISBN: Paperback 978-1-955070-30-0
       Hardback   978-1-955070-31-7
       Ebook   978-1-955070-32-4

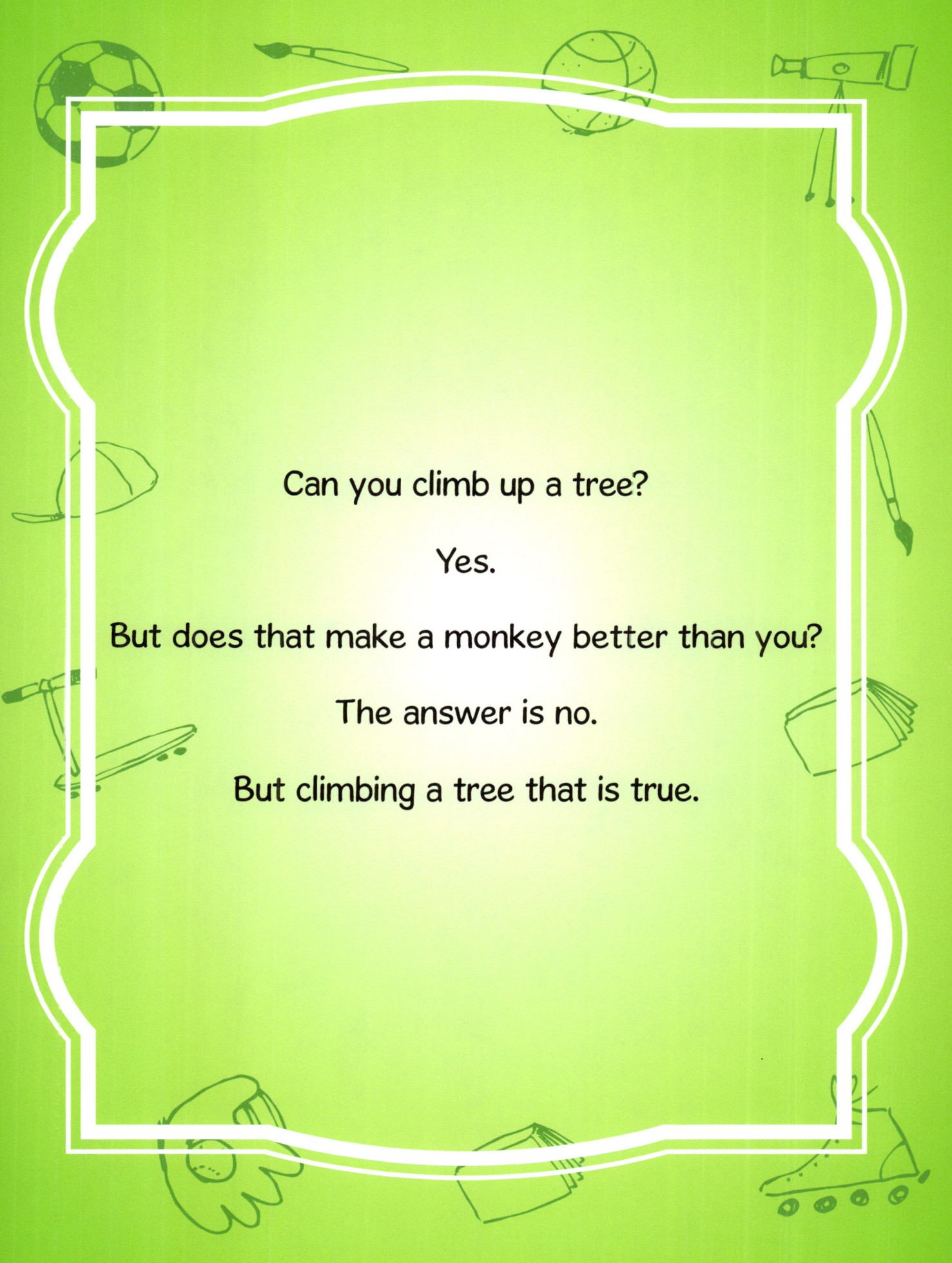

Can you climb up a tree?

Yes.

But does that make a monkey better than you?

The answer is no.

But climbing a tree that is true.

Can you swim in lakes?

Yes you can but a fish a better swimmer makes.

Does that make a fish better than you?

The answer is "no",

But in swimming that is true.

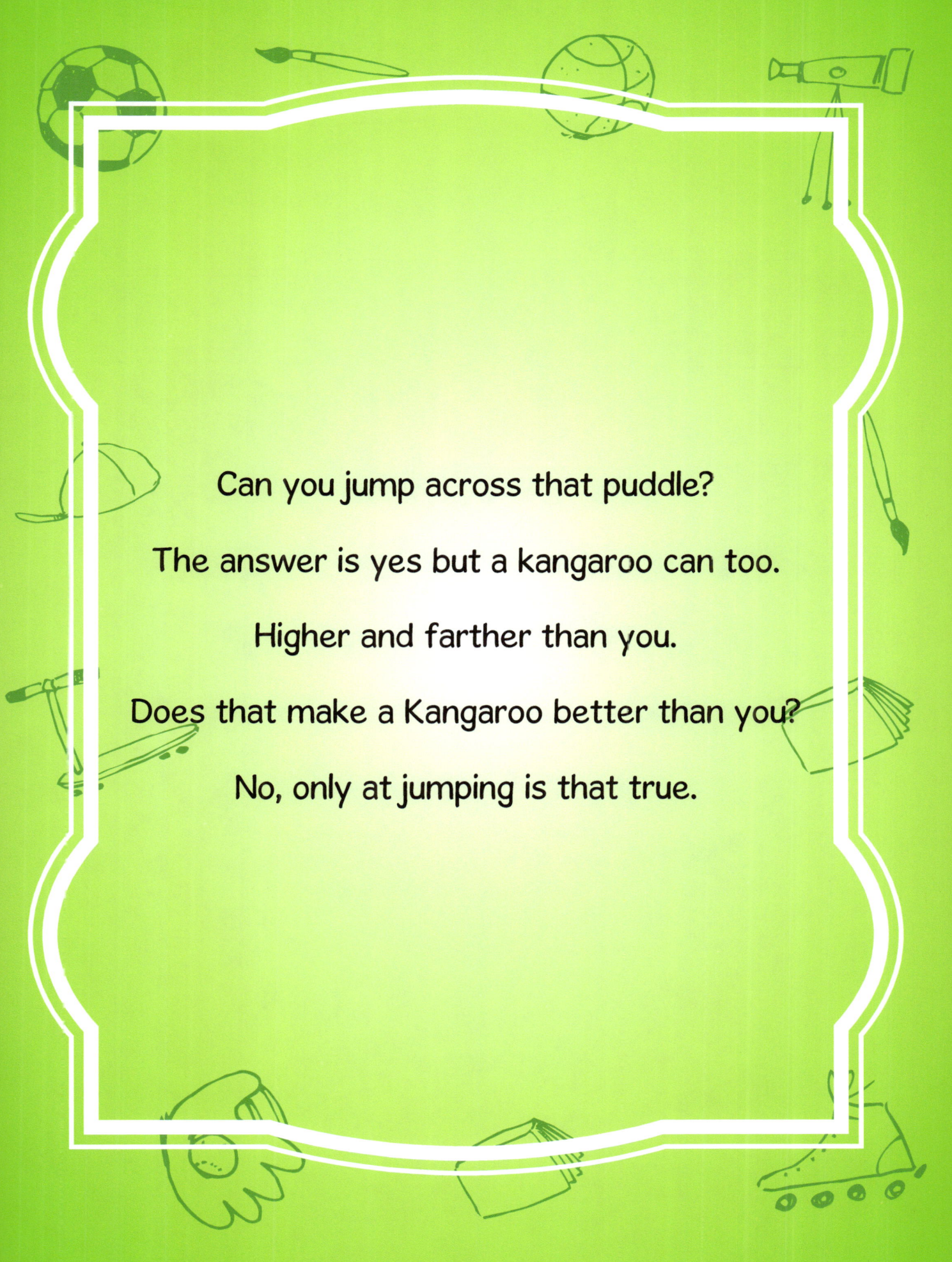

Can you jump across that puddle?

The answer is yes but a kangaroo can too.

Higher and farther than you.

Does that make a Kangaroo better than you?

No, only at jumping is that true.

Can you run a race?

Yes.

But a horse can run at a faster pace.

Does that make a horse better than you?

No. But at racing that is true.

Can you fly?

No.

A bird can and so can you.

In an airplane that is true.

Higher, faster, farther too.

To far away places like Disney Land.

Lucky, lucky, lucky you.

Can you play the kazoo?

Yes.

But some others may be more talented

in playing a musical instrument.

Does that make them better than you?

No. But playing a musical instrument is that true.

Enjoy their playing and congratulate them.

Lucky, lucky, lucky you.

Can you fly a kite?

Yes.

But others may be able to fly theirs at a higher height.

Does that make them better than you?

No but flying a kite that is true.

You might congratulate them and enjoy the sight.

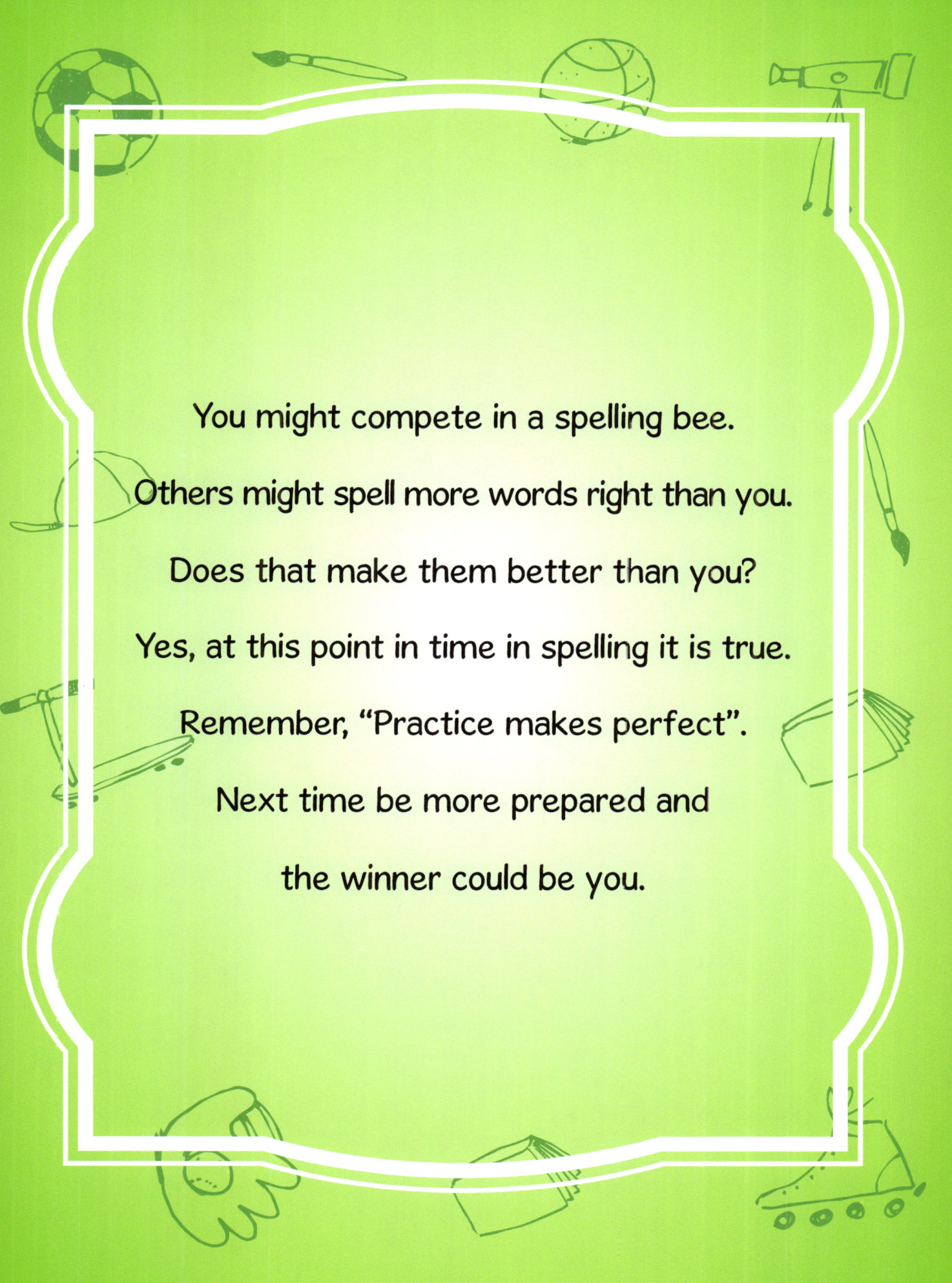

You might compete in a spelling bee.

Others might spell more words right than you.

Does that make them better than you?

Yes, at this point in time in spelling it is true.

Remember, "Practice makes perfect".

Next time be more prepared and

the winner could be you.

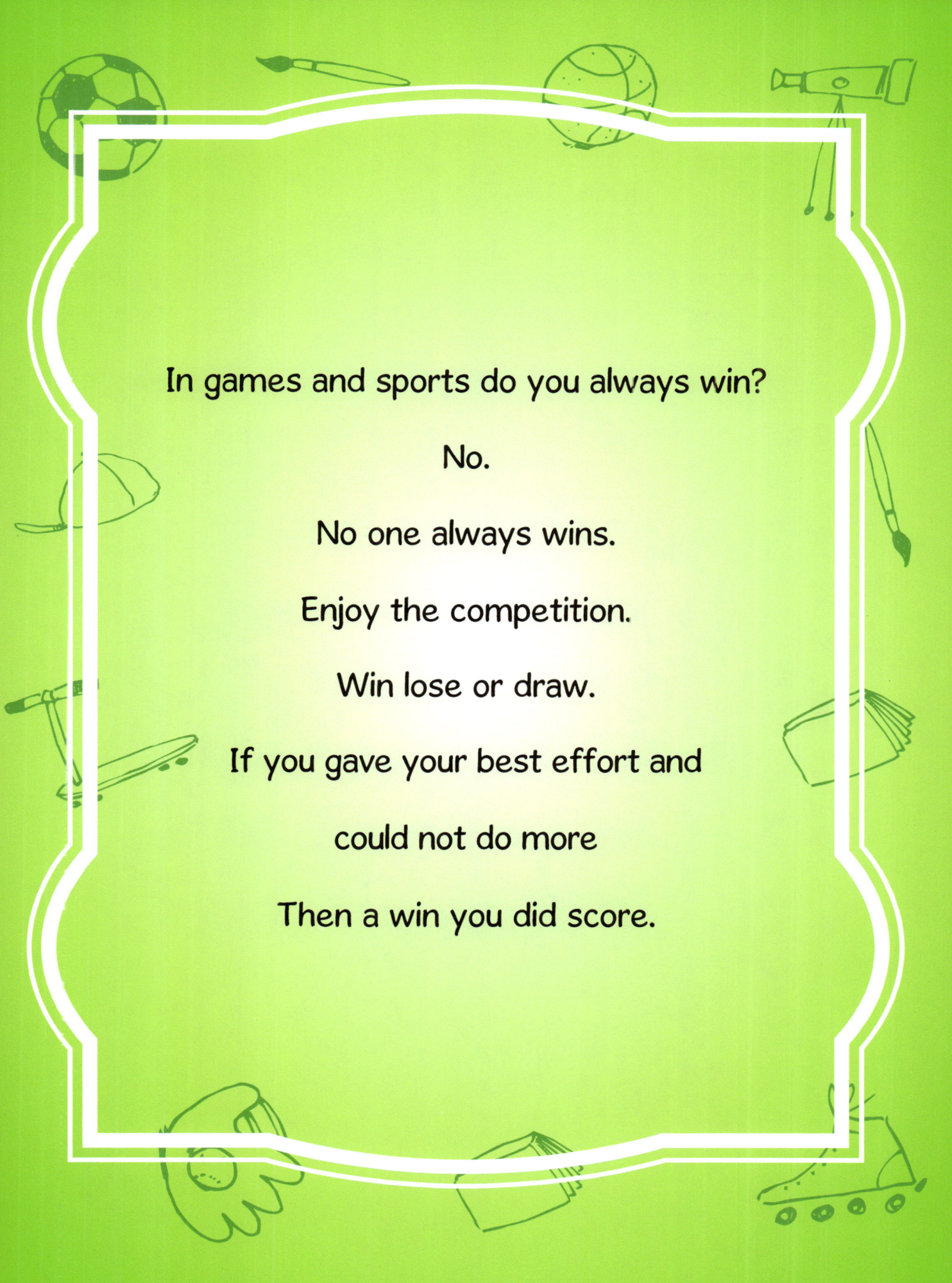

In games and sports do you always win?

No.

No one always wins.

Enjoy the competition.

Win lose or draw.

If you gave your best effort and

could not do more

Then a win you did score.

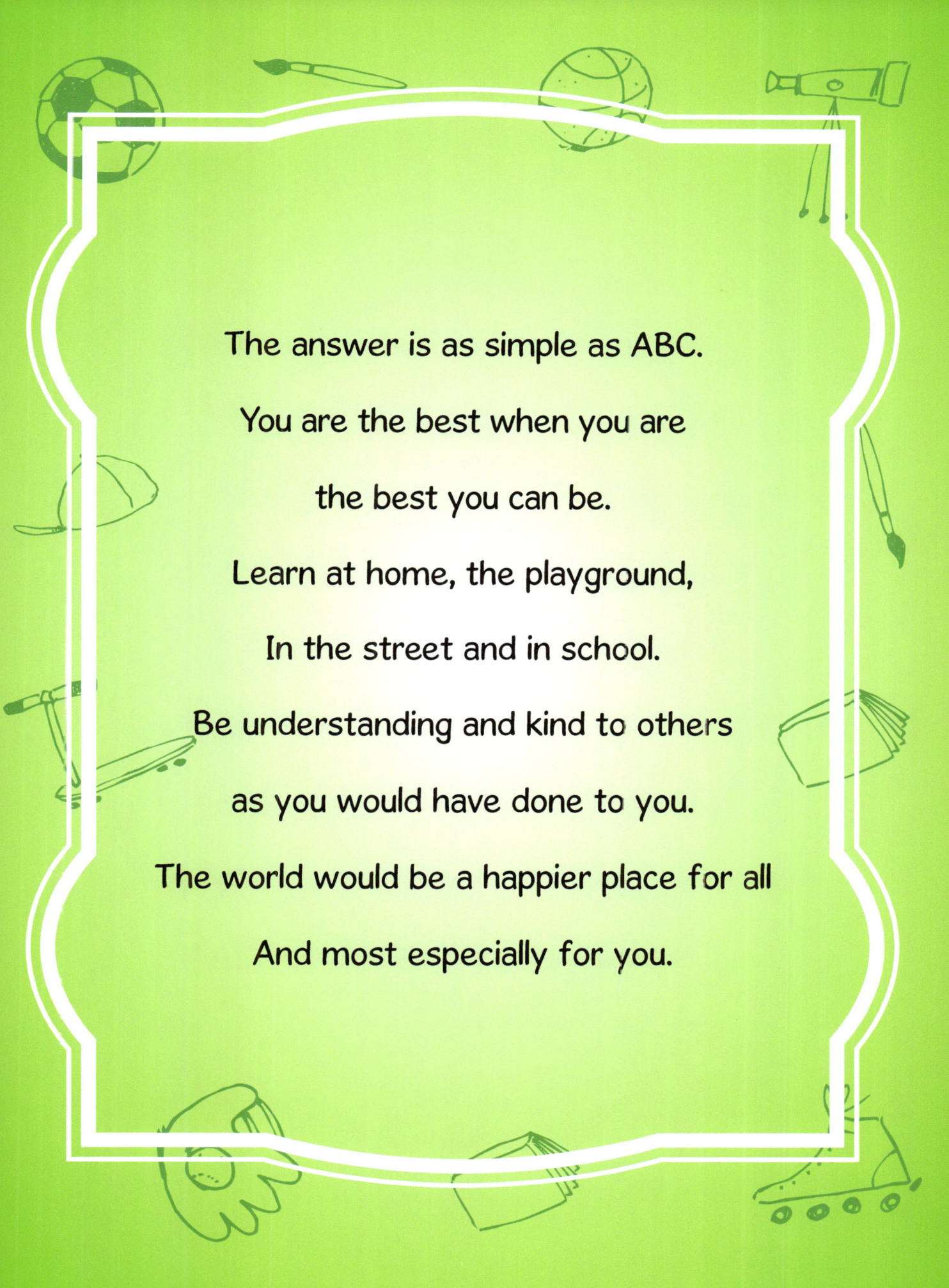

The answer is as simple as ABC.

You are the best when you are

the best you can be.

Learn at home, the playground,

In the street and in school.

Be understanding and kind to others

as you would have done to you.

The world would be a happier place for all

And most especially for you.

www.ingramcontent.com/pod-product-compliance
Lightning Source LLC
Chambersburg PA
CBHW041613120626
46551CB00002B/431